Volume 117 of the Yale Series of Younger Poets

Mass for Shut-Ins

Mary-Alice Daniel

Foreword by Rae Armantrout

Yale
UNIVERSITY PRESS
New Haven and London

PUBLISHED WITH ASSISTANCE FROM
A GRANT TO HONOR JAMES MERRILL.

Yale University Press books may be purchased in quantity for educational, business, or promotional use. For information, please e-mail sales.press@yale.edu (U.S. office) or sales@yaleup.co.uk (U.K. office).

Set in Yale type by Motto Publishing Services.
Printed in the United States of America.

Library of Congress Control Number: 2022942898
ISBN 978-0-300-26800-3 (hardcover : alk. paper)
ISBN 978-0-300-26799-0 (paper : alk. paper)

A catalogue record for this book is available from the British Library.

This paper meets the requirements of
ANSI/NISO Z39.48-1992 (Permanence of Paper).

10 9 8 7 6 5 4 3 2 1

MASS FOR SHUT-INS

manifested in 2012
during my tour of the Fox TV studios in Detroit.
Coming upon a set staging a Catholic program,
"Mass for Shut-Ins," I was baffled by the archaic nomenclature
used to brand Sunday services for home viewers.

lucubrationes
feminine noun

night work

"activities that take place by lamplight—sex, certainly, but also the other great adventures of the nighttime: doubt, prayer, melancholy, crime"

—Parul Sehgal

Contents

Foreword

"Hallelujah is the wrong word to begin so start over," writes Mary-Alice Daniel in her poem "Feel Better." Stark and uncompromising statements like that are the hallmark of her poetry. Unsparing and exacting, she dares the reader to accept the proposition that things *are* as bad as they seem. No consoling "but" follows. The five sections of *Mass* present evidence drawn from the many places in which Daniel grew up and spent time: Nigeria, the American South, Los Angeles—and, of course, the internet. Whichever way she looks she sees our "crazy baby steps to mass extinction." A sentiment this grim might be hard to tolerate if it wasn't accompanied by an original sensibility and a good ear. The last line I quoted is powerful because it slams the common, encouraging saying "baby steps" up against "extinction." (Baby steps *away* from extinction wouldn't help us now, let alone toward it.)

There is also a strong rhythm, a ghost of meter in many of Daniel's lines. When she calls out "One [who] downgrades bodies to zero status / & wakes up whistling *Dixie*," I notice that all the multisyllabic words in these lines contain two syllables with the accent on the first. These lines are not quite trochaic, but close enough. Say it out loud. One syllable added or taken away would detract. Notice too how attention is drawn to the words with the alliterated letter *d: downgrades* and *Dixie*. These are the most charged and significant words here. They suggest without saying so directly that the "downgraded" bodies are Black. Then is this a book about racism? No, not entirely, though that is certainly one of the evils Daniel has in her sights.

The poems in the book are divided into five sections, each preceded by a specially designed warning sign. The first untitled section, introduced by a generic caution sign, groups together poems named for moons—"Bloodmoon," "Wolfmoon," and "Ode to Our Unnamed Moon"—and poems dealing with the supernatural. Spells, demons, totems, and revivals make appearances. In the penultimate poem in the section, "Ode to Our Unnamed Moon," Daniel calls this "insurance against a God who seems to be 'seeing how things go.'" This spiritual stew comes naturally to Daniel, who was raised in syncretic Christian and Islamic traditions with a contribution from her Nigerian grandmother's animism. She reaches into these various belief systems as if looking for help in a world out of control, but, ultimately, remains skeptical.

The second section, titled "Anti-Noir (Series)," is preceded by a symbol against the evil eye common in the Islamic world. It is set in Los Angeles, an "indifferent paradise" threatened by "the Big One" and filled with serial killers and disaster tourists eager to be there when the San Andreas slides again. "Please publicize," Daniel writes, in a line I find telling and hilarious, "how I joked with the dead through dance." (Perhaps this is an Angeleno version of whistling past the graveyard?)

The universal symbol for radioactivity precedes an untitled section set mostly in Nigeria and featuring the various plagues prevalent there: TB, AIDS, malaria. One poem tells the story of an uncle who contracts AIDS in a dentist's office. Another recounts the story of the great-great-grandfather who was cut loose by slavers after they discovered he had leprosy. The biohazard symbol precedes "Mefloquine Side Effects (Series)." Mefloquine, which, Daniel tells us, is the most commonly used medicine for malaria in the region, is a perfect example of a cure that's worse than (or at least as bad as) the disease. It lists psychosis as a not uncommon side effect. The poems in this section have titles like "Nightmare," "Recurring Nightmare" and "Why Dream Logic Always Works against You." Is it ironic that we are so often the foils and victims of our own dreams, our own creations? Is it an instance of dramatic irony when the dreaming self knows what the waking self refuses to see?

One of the things I find most interesting about this book is that I sometimes find it difficult to distinguish between intended irony and plain observation. I hear something subtly ironic in this line, "Massive ships carry massive ships to ship/graveyards," though it could also pass for matter of fact. When overdevelopment comes to nothing, is that ironic? Are these container ships or war ships? Does it matter? It's an example of what's happening to and in the "developed" world now—the mass production of toxic obsolescence. Another example might be "Performance art collectives draped in ghostwear." I love the neologism "ghostwear." I assume it refers to sheets, such as ghosts were once portrayed as wearing, draped over the artifacts of some art "happening." This line too, like the one about the ships, evokes obsolescence, but here it's cultural fashions that are cycled through and abandoned. We too, Daniel suggests, are being fitted for our ghostwear, bound for the museum's basement. Is the joke on us?

Daniel has a good eye for the cracks and discrepancies in our worlds. She sees what's wrong, where the fault is likely to slip. Moreover, it seems to me, she grasps human psychology exceptionally well. That is, she sees how we fool ourselves, how we fiddle while the world burns: "The IKEA Effect: *if you assemble it, you love it.* / This cognitive error even applies to dreams." There are many ways *not* to recognize how bad a thing is. For instance, you can compare and contrast. As she says, "I suspect you mean to tie each desert / you've seen to another desert you have seen." The Sahel and the Mojave, perhaps. Similes and semblances are inherently reassuring. Thing B is like thing A, something with which we're already familiar. Comparisons make us feel we grasp and can thus control a thing—even if the thing is desertification and understanding does not lead to action. But Daniel won't take comfort: "Seeing mischief's next move, I hit my prey stride."

The fifth and final section opens with the symbol for flammable materials. The poems in this part are explorations of the nature and location of hell. I have no idea of Mary-Alice Daniel's ideas about the afterlife, but this book leads me to believe she has a good sense of the nature of hell on earth. ("Learn that life is a terrible wrath to pass down!") I see *Mass for Shut-Ins* as a gauntlet thrown down. What if things *are* as bad as they look (climate disasters, widespread wars, racial hatred, misogyny, and murder)? And what if blame can be placed not so much somewhere as almost everywhere—on our endless capacity for selfishness and cruelty? As the horror movie has it, "The call is coming from inside the house." This book might itself be seen as fatalistic and even perversely "dark." Daniel has inarguably spent a lot of time studying human viciousness and folly. The result is a *Flowers of Evil* for the twenty-first century. (I was happy to learn that Baudelaire was one of the first poets Daniel loved and learned from.) Frank O'Hara famously said, "You just go on your nerve." That is precisely what Mary-Alice Daniel does in this bold debut.

Rae Armantrout

Mass for Shut-Ins

MUST BE SOME KIND OF SPELL

Your favorite knife goes missing.
A guest stole something.

(Your house isn't haunted—you're just lonely.)

Walking through after the after-party,
see empty chairs in expert mimicry of human exercise:

assembling in conclave, two to four.
Facing conversation and cold cuts, policing every exit.

Sticky ring-stains sit beneath bottles all over your house,
concentric cones of hospitality radiating out in crop circles . . .

They are visual traps.
Also, they are sensory traps.
Also, they are fetishes.
They are effigy.

(Objects are animate.)

They want to return, like children or brides, to their owners.
A boning blade has vanished—the mojo in a home disturbed.

It turns up weeks later, under the precise center of your bed.
In that spot children hide from their parents' frantic reaching:

KNIFE

pointing perfect, straight at your pillow.

TOTEM

A screw in my motel room wall bothered me, and I couldn't get it out.

Even after using a t-shirt for leverage, it wouldn't budge.

Okay, so try a spell— *But realize—*

You cannot un-turn what you didn't yourself turn.
It's no matter that you drove alone to New Orleans,
bringing back an apothecary full of what you found.
No wonder no one lit those lucky candles you tried to gift.

I swear whoever first fixed the screw was no human.
Maybe he got booted out of every other job to have—
a night custodian wearing humanface over the body
of void that walks like us.

A screw in the port of call my great-great-grandfather would have disembarked—
if they hadn't pulled him off the slave ships when they culled lepers.

They sent him home, untouchable in the sugarcane, those slavers
moonlighting as missionaries— middlemen of the Middle Passage—

We want a papaya-and-brimstone Messiah: bushman and gentleman.
We want that part of the Bible where Black people get stoned.
We want our great revival with high caliber weapons,
Jesus looming over all holidays.

The screw held, and it never occurred to me to just leave it alone

or else become like songbirds making their headstrong way home—
Southbound; Temperate; Warbling

that manageable levels of the South shall rise again . . .

BLOODROOT

I've been trying to get it down—
what I mean when I think
back to Southern Melancholy.
You can see it in our old story charts
and in the radio short about a barefoot boy
who tried buying his way outta Appalachia,
selling bloodroot a buck a pound.

Here is the Cumberland River.

Here a strain of the heartsickness bubbling
through it, and so through childhoods.
Still I don't know many love songs, yet
I learned two names for each tree.
Alaqua—sweet gum. Chinquapin—
chestnut. Serviceberry—amelanchier.
One blackberry winter, I went
behind our apartment and down
the slippery ravine in flip-flops
(Blue Ash saplings saved my life)
just to touch what it was
that flooded, killing twenty.
What, once, when I was ten,
as if to confirm existence
of a petty/personal god,
claimed a neighbor's porch set,
which I did envy.

What could have stuck in these hills to make
the Scots-Irish accent drawl out—and twang
like certain strains in certain songs?

Expository musics of the same sad stone:
The Baptist Church. The other churches.
Pentecostal in the major days of diablerie.
Fleeing the root of rapture. Coming back,
always coming back. The call of the night
collector. The spectrum of the Bell Witch.
To make it more personal, I will elaborate.
If there must be a tornado, make it a fire whirl!
Feral as the Supercell that tore a Ford-shaped hole in the water tower.
We shielded our heads with slavery-apologetic textbooks—
those who knew to hide under underpasses
hid under underpasses.

REVIVALISM 101

You never wonder what demons do in downtime.
They're flat characters, not hobbyists.

But once, under a revival tent in Advent, it came out—
Keymakers, the preacher said.

Goldbeaters. Machinists. Weavers, Welders, Menders.

You should have figured only a Paperhanger could
wall in dreams with doodles of precancerous parents.

Only a Taxidermist could handle a corpse long after
you questioned why the fat heart hadn't given out—

heart that must have been skeined with dark, wrong veins:
liver sequined with syphilis.

Under the weight of perfection,
the Craftsmen set to their task in studio and playroom—

Whip and *Grump* and *Immolation* and *Work,*
nothing at all about worrying the same old things over and over:

> *...Sometimes, I imagine I can tell by a girl's name:*
> *how or how much her parents love her—proposing*
> *there's never been an unloved Ibis, Hasbiya, Little*
> *Laughing Dove—names of birds, never of flowers.*

And how they are masterful—these practiced, relentless Ones—
grand hydra architecture of contamination & cooperation.

While our own world destroys itself, all *we* do is eat, sleep, groom.
Or write obsessively about bodies as objects of death study.

SLIPSTREAM

Like Kamikazes, houseflies dive-bombing my wine
—*(six have wasted themselves to dim Shiraz liquidity)*—
pitch waves of special force attacks and turn
bellies to sun in self-murder.

Unlike Kamikaze pilots, they have not written death
poems and care too much, I think, for Muscovado.
These could be stories we sell milk-slick children
to warn them from balcony edges.

* * *

Ask anyone who plays around with planes on weekends.
They'll tell you: propeller accidents are not abnormal.
Really, the most remarkable thing about Shari's case:
She lives. Putting her back together produced a patent.

The tarmac confetti was pieces of map on pieces of thumb.
This suggests she did *not* intend to walk just there.
Within the whir of three broad blades—angel wings
as they approach imperceptible—she surprised herself.

But how could she neglect insistent wind in the slipstream?

Perhaps she'd been looking down at her sky charts.
Perhaps bowing to offer routine prayer in preflight.
Perhaps that frustration—stuck inside one whole body,
one bone-house abiding one place at a time.

What if she just wanted to feel strange mechanics in motors?
You must remember: Curiosity and Satisfaction are primal—

Primal. Basic. Stone Age. Reptilian.

FEEL BETTER

There are some among us with no impulse control I mean zero
Give them a pencil they stick it in their eye

Show a picture of eyelash mites no eyelashes seconds later
You strap them in a wheelchair crazy as hallelujah

Useless meat puppet carnival of animals
No wonder cannibals label us long pigs not purely for taste

Little Chayya in India worried the world would die
when the Large Hadron Collider rebooted

She thought earth would crack up and everyone on it
would get pulled like a body just getting pulled

Scientists as ever warning nothing to fear calm yourselves calm calm
But a black hole   What a bad end

The rabble rushes to temple Chayya runs from evening news
straight to the bleach you already guessed she chugged it

Hallelujah is the wrong word to begin so start over
Tiny tiny crazy baby steps to mass extinction

BLOODMOON

Our moon should tip over

into the gulf.

Bad apple in a pool, it is that big &
unbalanced & ultimate beyond material.
We pass the dead-point of marginal sea
praying God lays Hands on top of our plane
to stop us from shooting up into the exosphere . . .

THIGMOTROPIA:
every creature obeys the impulse to ensconce itself–

think of vermin cozying your walls
and the audacity in their desire,
the plain directive of life
toward comfort.

PSYCHOTROPIA:
that incantation driving you out of your head–

many ways to cut it,
but at the heart,
a knife fight.

You are an outsider scientist on a shoestring budget,
trawling sky for timber or townships on the moon,
for the moon circuses dead men sought,
back when we believed in counter-earth.

See for yourself–

We must be heading Somewhere. Somewhere,
there must be force pushing the thing forward.
Our moon oppressing, overworking waves to spittle.
In submission to a satellite overripe, the world bends.

At this size, a moon in bloom.

It cradles. It is orange.

WOLFMOON*

What the hell is a *wolfmoon*?*
We don't need more types of moon.
We just need a better moon.
One that gives more room.

Moondogs appear when full-moon-light pierces ice crystals,
parading a pair of mock moons astride the one true moon.
They occur in Arctic climates—also in African imagination.
Zambia, 1964: where to witness the spectacle of Afronauts.
In unfunded ambition to outdo America & the Americans,
a teacher supposes he can argue with all applicable omens.

His catapult will send to the moon and Mars a spacegirl
+ her pets, well-trained inside oil drums tossed downhill.
More bodies circle the drain of a Great Stratospheric Sink.
The dogs recruited for early and eccentric space programs:
strays in a wild love with Soviet steak and marijuana.
(CUE: mist, howl of wolf, nest of mink.)

Canine suicides off a bridge pile like junk mail—*(fifty!)*—
tenacious and acrobatic, all long muzzles in the mornings:
then the lone, disabled one in a steaming pool in Houston.
A sub-orbital mutt, if exceptional, survives 12 flight hours.
We look up at our moon and might see our star
in a malevolent, dog-headed saint.

Politically, I believe in revenge raining down from outer space . . .

ODE TO OUR UNNAMED MOON

MOON and its dark star of calamity
MOON like moths: twilight- and night- flying white moths
MOON with half-suicidal/half-sexual affect

Unimpressed, Islamic councils won't standardize a lunar calendar.
Should we bother to name it soon? A Copernican principle insists
there is nothing super special about Earth's cruddy corner of universe:

moon *star* *sunshine* *everything* *else*

Yet in our orbit, Neil Armstrong claims he heard the call to prayer—
the Adhan—thus converting. First man bowing from Moon to Mecca.
Did he think to recheck his horoscope? Astrology is anthropocentric:

Constellations appear entirely different anywhere other than Earth—
Pick any moon; Planet that is a diamond; Planet of inaudible hum.
Tethered to a planet of escalating nonsense, I try homemade kismet.

I run a Random Bible Verse Generator and turn scripture into policy.
Call it insurance against a God who seems to be "seeing how things go."
Personally, I believe prophecy only if it fits: *neatly inside the nonzodiac.*

ILL-STARRED

In animatronic tones, Tina Luckless turns on me.
So she says to me, she says to me, she says:

I wanna hotwire a blue '57 Chevy—but just to take it
once around the block before returning it where it was.

Tired of delusions, I say this is too specific.

We are driving down Main Street in my truck.
It hit 200,000 miles and takes a calamity to turn over.

It is the holiday season, so trees dress in moonbows & firebows.
They glitter and shatter in a washpoint of starshower.

They surprise.   They find me afraid.

How her voice turns metallic—Now her eyes are painted on—
black as oil spill or oil beetle. I am afraid if sanity's a choice,

of what in this room I might use to hurt myself and others,
the lack of proper barricading between Us and Empty Space.

Early warning systems had a very serious influence
on the formation of my whole heart.

But what was it my mother always used to say?

Don't whistle into the dark. You will surely draw devils here . . .

And what am I doing now but whistling.

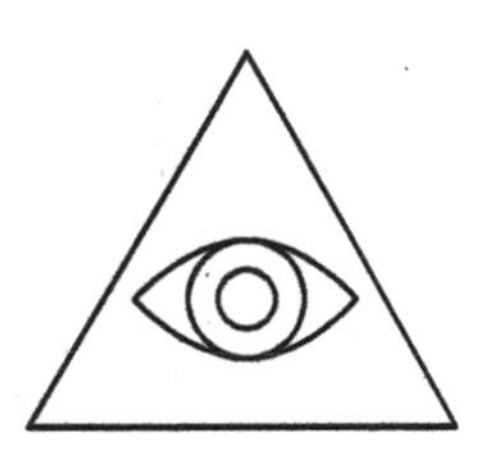

ANTI-NOIR

SERIES

NOLLYWOODLAND

for the actress terrified of aging

Imagine doing Hollywood with a phobia of light.
Faring fluorescence along La Brea, shy on Sunset.
Despairing of this desert where a defect in scorpions
makes them glow and reflect moonlight, starlight.

Navigating night via dung beetles, who in turn steer
by the imprecise & petty light from our Milky Way.
Meanwhile, Lucifer—Light Bringer, Morning Star—
seeks whom he may devour.

You're exposed in Technicolor outside every 99¢ store,
unmasked in the alright yellowing at early bird events.
By matinée and marquee. Vintage & Space Age neons.
Bad energy adds up in glossy infrastructure of unluck.

So, flee to Nollywood—

to Nigeria's daily power outages and the mercy in kerosene.
Just stay hidden during the dawning hours, and safe away
from alchemies of equatorial light steeped with all sunrise.
On the Dark Continent: *Night is coming, when one can work.*

The Vatican formally declared the death saint Santa Muerte
blasphemous, so pray to any patron saint of total lost causes.
Pray to sink into tar pits and transform fully into the fossil
you are already becoming . . . enshrined eons later in Lucite . . .

HAGIOGRAPHY OF A PILLAR OF SALT

The Tourism Board of Jordan
still searches for extrusions of salt
resembling one fallen woman.
Lot's Wife, she may be styled—
or Ado or Edith or the female Orpheus.

In make-believe metropolis: God & Evil live a mile apart.
A sinful woman is told to flee the city of her addictions
and go where good people go.

She drops dead crossing this journey's exact midpoint.
Angels and demons bicker in the borderland—one side
complaining she didn't travel far enough to earn herself:

[*So, burn.*]

The other faction protesting that the act of going proved
her intentions—as if Salvation should work by proximity,
or Sanctuary as circles of protection defying zoning codes.

God tells them to measure the precise distances between
Sin City . . . Her Body . . . & The Place of Redemption.
[We'll call this place *Los Angeles*—for the angels of good.]

Perhaps He makes her body fall west,
which is Best. I like to think God extends civic boundaries
out to corpses in obvious parallel: to suburbia, its sprawl.

The people of paradise and the principalities of hellfire—
between them: half-lost quarrels with gods. Worst of all,
Hell was prepared and waiting before poor man was born.

DEATHCENTRIC

City in sinister pattern—pulsing in and out of gridlock.
A little give, a little take, slow cruise through the wreck.
Decide quick whether it's *scared* or *lethal* you need to be.

The type of disaster townies and transplants volunteer
to risk tells you something about the point of that place.
Mad science manipulating seismic activity can't save us:

Of many American options, Angelenos stay ready to die
beside freaky blue flashes often sighted during quakes,
knowing the plates beneath are waiting—willing to shift.

{Subculture of specter.}
{El Doradan Optimism undercut by fault line.}
{Like blinking the instant an overhead light goes out.}

One who came to dig for gold departed against all odds
with bullion for his bride and black sand in baby's name.
Gone five years, he found every family member he'd left

still alive, and not a single brother in jail. Luck is mined in
goldfields—is made of miracles that will not leave us alone.
We're all still having babies here, but we spay/neuter pets.

Who will come along with us casually to death's deep end?
We who know nothing of snowflakes the size of milk pans.
Let's look forward to that feeling when the Big One stuns—

Rude Ravens Frolic in Snow Like Children

CHAOS MUPPET

A. Aftershocks of the Great Mexico City Earthquake rocked me in utero.
As a statuette of Mary nodded *YES*, seizing against the wall
before falling, my mother predicted I would bring fortune
(80% of divination starts with shit falling to the ground).

B. If I take advantage of another disaster and disappear,
I've fled town to make a new life. Such is a practice
repeated the world over by women disappointed–
by the children or money, their fathers' country.

C. Seeing mischief's next move, I hit my prey stride.
I will start over suffering the sadness of knowing
I'll never know how the human timeline turns out.
In this batshit state where fake IDs are semi-legal–

I'm a thin woman, there is a beach, etc.

D. My Philosophy of Fear professor anticipated
these nights of trouble appointed me.

Getting scared just for fun
feeds our last primeval urge.
We have nothing much left
to worry about, no tigers
at the mouths of our huts.
What would you do if Hell
broke through this door?
You couldn't fight
one frantic child.

E. I have none to comfort me amongst my lovers—
All my friends have dealt treacherously with me.
I'm the woman asking what it means about her:
that she sees a greasy handprint on the window,
a little larger than her own paws, and whimpers,
wondering what made it.

F. GOOD NEWS!

The murder of Kitty Genovese was misreported,
and the bystander effect might not be that bad.

Cataclysm, come after me . . .
Perfect strangers may help.

MURDERABILIA

Of ______ active American serial killers,
three-quarters call this *Home* and *happy hunting*—
livable ghostland, redlike, in photochemical fog.
Lots leading out nowhere, people all chased off,
that man in his hole by the party store.

A pilgrimage of predators, drawn west.
Jack the Journalist came to expose California crime
then killed 3 prostitutes in homage to his subject.
To move such an audience, you must write coldly:
A parking ticket is not atrocity—no matter how unjust.

Setting up the center of bad industry,
camera crews hack knots of iconic buried creatures.
Big body count of Carnivora. Apocalypse a little bit.
Crime tethers us to people & places we really need
to get away from.

LINE DO NOT CROSS POLICE LINE DO NOT CROSS POLICE LINE DO NOT CROSS

Those at the end of their rope, in turn,
end lives. It's just what people do here.
The estimate of undetected murders
in history is called our *Dark Figure*—
magnitudes we make flesh
in the death-dealing past,
in the *soft-shoe* of
killing still.

POLICE LINE DO NOT CROSS POLICE LINE DO NOT CROSS POLICE LINE DO NOT

INDIFFERENT PARADISE

In the likely case I die soon in the city first called
El Pueblo de Nuestra Señora la Reina de los Ángeles,
you can feel superior that way we do whenever
we hear of an acquaintance dying young.

Historians will never agree on the original name,
but settlers intended angels; that much we know.
Neither can we agree on our official public saint—
wish me *Godspeed* escaping this Earth & its pull.

If I die scuffling in a fixed-income residential hotel,
pray to Christina the Astonishing against insanity.
If I die of the usual—light today, dull tonight—
try Pio of Stress Relief: martyr of new year blues.

If when I go, I am still more a *saddy* than a *baddy,*
pester Chad of Mercia, charged to protect losers.
Incense in all cases, in pirate attacks, for Albinus.
If I die in techno-sized unreality, in social disaster,

in superheated parking lots amid the blasts of smut
terrorizing The Town of Our Lady Queen of Angels,
where we finally heard from the raving-man-ghost
and celebrities huddle to mourn Marius the Giraffe—

You must remember how cities become cities . . .
Corpses create this. Crime scenery and killing field.

When the Health Department holds its annual burial
for the unclaimed dead, honoring 1547+ indigents
whose remains share storage space in our county crypt,
take care not to mistake me for my body double, then—

unearth me.

ADIOS, LA . . .

Please publicize how I joked with the dead via dance.
If there was kindness involved.
How the melodramatic universe hurt me and must pay.

Memorialize me using *cinemagraphs:*
otherwise still photos
with minor, repeating movement

(tiny movement)
(endless loop)
(Tantalusian)

A single frame:
(me playing with a rose in my teeth)
(welcoming you into the machine of light)

Meaningful background graffiti:
<3 let time come and eat itself <3
DEATH WILL BE YOUR SANTA CLAUS

Suffer the frustration
of photographing something amazing
knowing a million similar shots already exist

&

Wherever I die,
name that place after me—
whatever loosely translates to:

*"death trundling along a ramshackle Purple Line
out to Fukushima-tainted waters"*

MEAN WORLD SYNDROME*

**a pattern of perceiving the world as more dangerous than it is*

All industry as we set out for Hausaland. Then green and green.

Greening all over the windows—this is the rabid brush, *Nigeriana.*

The Slave Coast highway system gives shantytowns something to do,

and our "Pearl of Tourism" features gold rush & holy mess.

But if we pass one more "Blood of Jesus Barber Shop," *I'm done.*

If we pass one more shape looking utterly as it should.

—GIANT MOON—BIG BEAR OF A MOON—A FRIGHTENING LOOM—

Such wonderworking within our Earth-Moon-Sun scheme,

such happy science. Plus Coincidence. Plus Catastrophe.

A whole airplane wing dragged behind a truck one lane over:

Hurt locomotion. Large amputation thing.

Never seen anything like it, so it makes the day.

And then you see another . . . and another . . .

(I told you: Objects are animate.)

They think of retreat, like soldiers to the seat of their caliphate.

Enter the place of stopped bodies— *Water, the weapon of war.*

Come for white skies . . . good food . . . bad blood.

MIAMI WORLD SYNDROME

INNOCENT NIGERIANA

(returning to a place after 11 years,
after an uncle's 3rd wife bit the ear off his 2nd –
thus the feud that drove aunts to airport lounges,
calling us in England, asking what shall they do)

The carpet as the same carpet.
The children are like children.
Dogs *Pavlov* to other language,
and what was a house is a table of water.

The big reveal of which given names
against infant mortality work best.
Plus a beehive beneath seats of the Citroen.
We settle in Tin City on the cold plateau–

where grow custard apples and
bloated plastic bags of bacteria.
Frost wipes out 45 chicks in one bite.
Amongst other predator issues–

jackal situation, golden caracal fiasco.
the radio-tracked male, tracking.
the female hiding carcasses in trees.
a tiny maniac, such as a child.

Flies with their classic behavior of over-
involvement. Men pray in the umbrage
of medium mountains for daughters,
girls who belong wholly to mothers.

Each wedding, a girl wears a gown:
the custom of the little bride. As if
we alone were born below lucky stars,
here is adventure seeking edges under acid rain.

I learn that goats are afraid of thunder. All night,
the eldest butts her head against the kitchen door
trying to break in. The lesser bleat pathetically—
wanting to be let inside, certain they are human.

DISEASE MAP

It's about my aunt getting tuberculosis.
Outbreak in her village is *Devilry* after 1 death—*Risk* at 10.

You can reduce anything to a number and elevate any number
to a name: *Pandemic* at 100, when the W.H.O. trucks roll in.

Harbingers of infection are chickens, songbirds, and horses.
In TB cases, the first to die are slender birds learning to sing

the same way toddlers talk. A process of trying and flailing—
A fucked-up, un-birdlike song.

Otherwise, not much warning except general wrongness.
Hunger and nausea couple. On the disease map,

the wash of pink covering Sokoto State is impolite,
alluding too obviously to swollen gums.

I believe there are lifetime statistics that should be kept
on all of us: *How many times disease has saved your life.*

My great-great-grandfather was kidnapped as a slave
and released. He backtracked a borderline on leprous legs,

so tired his soul just dragged its body along on his shoulders—

back

and

back

to the ancestry of *Infection*.

VIOLENCE IS MOTHER AND DAUGHTER

I

There is a superstition
that holding a dying creature in adolescence
leaves the offender with trembling hands for life.
Perhaps some early bloodletting on my father's part
explains why all photos by his hand are blurred.

II

The photographs I return to
when I feel I could hate my mother—
Inside, insecurities condense into wet
hatred for my father and for America.
A boxing ring past ruin makes our stage
in sepia. She holds me up to prove how
well she can twist my hair with wire.
I am a baby with a pink Lamborghini
and selfish with birthday cake.
I'm forcefully posed—so, beginning
to understand the Will to Power.
Her expression: *You've made it. So what?*
You're old. I wish for something else—
images more happily complicated,
calligraphies in communal spaces,
as in their wedding album.
I am jealous of my father;
she is young and playful.
Or she is biting her bottom lip,
sort of sad. A box above her,
ORTHODYNAMIC HEADPHONES,
and a framed poem with words
I can't make out: 3 lines of what?

III

Just now, I am nearing the age she feared *then*—
that age people compulsively show off pictures
of parents. Same age a countdown commences:
How many times you will kiss her before she dies.
I grew up this way: one hand in my mouth
and the other on my mother's breast—
until I got too grown and she had to
fend me off. By 10, she'd broken me.
I used to draw her image in the cleaning closet
of the old house, before they were students,
when we were refugees. Illicit in between
Domestos Thick Bleach & minor toxicants,
I drew her as a pentagon. With a paint scraper,
I etched fancies: there she appears in series
of green damage. Notice attention to detail.
Notice absent father. Once I made 2 lines.
No one could figure out what they were.
She and I would flash in unison
—eyes looking more and more
red and rabbit—INFERNINA
meaning *little feminine Hell.*

FOR MY UNCLE
WHO DIED OF AIDS
CONTRACTED AT THE DENTIST'S OFFICE

If he dies during the Month of Brides it is a great shame.
Wash the body 3 or 5 or 9 times. Not 2 or 4 or 6 times.
We see Allah configuring candlesticks in the starry hall:
    laying a supergrid, unlaying it, and
    remixing the music of the situation.
    Widening cycles contain us within
    these compulsions as He wonders
    which fires He left un-extinguished.
Enter daymares of blank dogs devouring each other in play.
    Inner workings of afterlife . . . active yet odd.
Welcome all to mourning—Buddhist and born again,
    followers of Christ or Kali, ultra-black goddess
    of Time and Life and Doomsday and Death.
Harvest healthy organs. Into his grave, place no object.
Avoid sunrise, high noon, sunset. Avoid autopsy.
Who commits to us such opulent instruction?
    All-Holy, All-Subtle Author.
    Rich Absolute All-Provider.
    Upgrader & Ever-Reckoner.
The face must point toward the House of God in Mecca;
    those living walk beside or in front of death.
Tolerate neither embalming nor emotional outburst,
    for though we surrender our dead to the earth,
    forward from it
                    we shall bring them
                                once again.

The procedure described above is the only one correct.
To Him do we belong and unto Him must we return.

ZOMBI

i

just
had
a really
weird
moment
where
my mind
told me
to tell
your
mind–

infection
is a star
that
fell
inside
your
body

:

a
portal
to new
half-visual
body technology

(to transfer
bulk tissue
is surgery—
to shape it,
        art)

with broom of purification
soon comes Babalú-Ayé

(cripple god)
(our god of cholera)
(of AIDS & influenza)

    to score how
    well you live
    with malady

MEFLOQUINE SIDE EFFECTS

SERIES

LARIAM® (LAH-ree-am)
Generic: mefloquine hydrochloride

Mefloquine is a prophylactic medication used to prevent and treat malaria. I take tablets weekly whenever I return to West Africa. It is notorious for inducing serious psychological side effects. Some who take mefloquine experience sudden yet severe mental problems: hallucinations, distressing dreams, panic, paranoia, disorientation, and derealization. Some consider or commit suicide. Its label warns of irregular behavior, irregular thought. Discontinue if you begin to lose touch with reality. Side effects may continue long after usage. One woman remained in mefloquine psychosis for months.

HYPERREALITY

1/ We are bound together in a substance called Pan-African Fire.

2/ Butterflies sputter like defueling generators.

3/ We say we are mercenary to murder mosquitoes.
One we let get away for that emotion most like pity
—*we thought it dying already*—and catch yellow fever.

4/ This may seem extreme etcetera, but mentally, it's the deal—

5/ Ants cutesy with their work ethic, in procession
to carry a cockroach over the troublesome ledge.
An ant is off-task, spiriting away a forewing.

6/ Liquor truly starts becoming the biggest thing.

7/ Doors make all kinds of sounds but this one just giggled.

8/ We each have a customized bacteria cloud around us at all times:

9/ *the creepy clusterfuck of body,*

10/ A Shocking Sabbath Carnival of Death.

11/ This whole country dislodges and swims off into oceans.

12/ Here comes trouble from the trouble people.

13/ Animal walking toward those people.

NIGHTMARE

The first thing the dead might say
when they finally get a chance to respond

is: *Sing!*

(*Terrible singing—terrible song.*)

The dead may be controversial—they may liken us to birds.
Maybe birds should go unmentionably wild.

Sometimes the spiritlike quality is pleasing and slight.
But once in a while, I want a little *muscle*—you know?

I don't feel the full weight of nest-robber broods
because birds are only wings, wings are only light.

Parrots do have presence.
They have the quality of bad visitants, a spooky nature in speech.

Crows remember funny faces—(*conspire*)—can find you.
Your body internalizes flight-coded lingo in dreams—

birdsong and black box, piping pilots' last words.
The two-inch feather erupts from a baby girl's neck.

RECURRING NIGHTMARE

The IKEA Effect: *if we assemble it, we love it.*
This cognitive error even applies in dreams.
One emerging psychiatric practice suggests
scripting nightmares to eliminate the worst.

Not everyone agrees it's healthy.
I only write nightmares of murder in a small town.
Looking for ideas, when I get my alumni magazine,
I immediately flip back to the Necrology—

too few, the new dead from graduating classes
of the 1930s, a decade petering out of life.
Then couplets of death give sudden way to stanzas—
It's not heartless to think of this as verse.

I used to trust my luck could only go up, spontaneously,
and never took that to the logical extreme: tumor.
I am interested in how dreams spiral—from the center—
a little or a lot each turn:

> *the victim incurs the wrath of fiends*
> *or else is chosen to become their horse.*

But maybe I should stop riling things up . . . ?

Hippasus was drowned at sea for theorizing irrational numbers.
That's seriously all it takes.

WHY DOES DREAM LOGIC ALWAYS WORK AGAINST YOU?

That murder may happen. That murder is the first resort.
That you are anticipated by whatever wants to overwhelm.
That if the witch in bed beside you climaxes—
Spells strengthen tenfold.

Occasionally, you will have only a notion liking the word "songster."

An infirm crowd occupies this adult education center:
milling around widowhood & phobia,
they're in the latter part of practical life.
Inside we sit – *so* – *still* – *so* – *senseless* –
the motion-detecting lights turn off.
A disembodied hand creeps through
for course evaluations: *Lights On*
Monks sit still for the camera as
they self-immolate: *Lights Off*

Enough Hamletting. In dreams, one needs grounding. A setting, that is—
Let's just pick a cabin where everything runs on fire: couch, dresser, TV.

I suspect you mean to tie each desert
you've seen to another desert you have seen,
supposing water is the same water everywhere.
But life is vortex, not rotation—your witch
softly speaking the flower language—

vulgar mind (marigold)
mental beauty (old man's beard)
i declare against you (belvedere)
i follow into dreams (orchid)
oh yes (pink)

Now she has powers in tens.
Metastructures of Hell grow masculine in mefloquine.
In terms of risk, the high forest high fire high flood zone of risk–

May flowers throw themselves before your feet

as if the devil is not
and yet

YOU REMAIN IN PSYCHOSIS FOR MONTHS

Take the drug religiously and catch malaria—you're riding the malarial wave—

Fever is the goat, it bleats:

you ate me, Mary-Alice / you wore a boot of me

and served the cheese of me to children

Road trips taken in high fever are different.
Every few miles, a human-related incident,
or Shiva trampling the dwarf of Ignorance
and tap-dancing the cosmos into existence.
The Midwest coming for the rest of your life . . .

What can you do about it now.

- In delirium, music by the Violin of Disgrace
  + testimonials for Teethfallingout.org

- On billboards, a gaggle of "greenbirds"
  exalting the nest of martyrs
  hung in chandeliers across the throne of the Almighty

- On every surface, 23 emotions we all feel but cannot name:

People are heartening, for example.
People are the actual, valid argument
against their abuses.

Your heart can't really explode. I mean,
I am sure it could.

AT LAST, ENTER THE CASTLE OF MENTAL & PHYSICAL WELLBEING

Instead—the whitening of a normalized canvas.

(the pale spectaculum in bones)

The low-key milk of bare wall & boring morning.

(calibrated to cute)

False pockets, which are the work of the current devils.

The mind the opposite of ink, as empty shopping cart.
Your cart soon full of God & Good Idea: conversations
on the logistics of lighting up plantations. About mass,

moving graves. About megasymptoms of misdemeanor
here within the sheer shambolics of a slavery economy,
leading back to a gigantic movement of American Evil.

Somehow, a singing of the good world each sunrise comes.

This we call – "DAY."

ENQUIRY INTO THE LOCATION & NATURE OF HELL

We all know what we think of Vultures.
We did not know they have shadow life.
We are deprived of 1 or many faculties.

Awaiting the long-promised appearance
of crane-necked and goose-necked men:
War, our only mode of house and home.

How we have to live in the middle stage
of ritual: meddlesome unicorns register
in the rare class of Things Never to Kill.

Of course, when it comes to Animalia—
always mistakes are made. Bible-colored
butterfly sets itself down clean on white

floors, no evident trauma, and just dies.
For the 352 active national emergencies,
send help. Prefaced by long fall and fire:

a sky *so grey*

even the stupid child knows it will rain.
We hum, gamble, break off into cliques.
Today is a day that could go either way . . .

ONE HELL

One for busybodies
One for frying chickens alive
One for crying aloud in the night
  at the beginning of night watches
One for eating sweets with rice

One for butterfly collecting
—god, what an evil hobby—
gassing living things to itemize
  in your hovel in England

One borderline

One-bedroom disaster mansion
One black hole & bad experiment
One romantic *Wow!* after another
One forest becomes abundantly fell

One *millihelen*, the quantum of beauty
    required to launch One warship

One snatches us from fairgrounds, wriggling, out . . .

One sifts you into aerosol . . .
    a spray of rose oil pretty as powder
    adrift within waves of radio water

One downgrades bodies to zero status
    & wakes up whistling *Dixie*

One is a killing jar—
    even calls itself that

One of One desire—
    eat every animal
    in God's Good Claymation

TWO HELL

Massive ships carry massive ships to ship
graveyards. Aircraft on back of aircraft.
Our construction of the Brooklyn Bridge,
cables eager to catch humans—

humans otherwise caught
in a net of telephone wire
humans assimilated into
the larger borg

A French Revolutionary politician gave
each day of the year its own true name.
Pitchfork. Maple Syrup. Silica. Scythe.
Barrel. Bedstraw. Dung. Crucible. Plague.

I've come to admire toned-down language
in manic habits of the monstrously lonely.
As I like the laid-back vernacular
scientists use for leviathan things:

VERY LARGE ARRAY *HUGE LARGE QUASAR GROUP*

THE BIG CRUNCH *THE WEAK FORCE*

NEWFOUND BLOB *EXTREMELY LARGE TELESCOPE*

SPAGHETTIFYING *GREAT DYING*

Nothing just IS anymore. Everything *Super* is.
On top of mainstream madness in planets:
Posthumans are more than biological.
*Plus*humans are typically 8 feet tall.

A billion brains symphonize in realtime.
Immaculate simulacrum of precisely one
cubic meter. And asteroid terrorism.
And slow-moving wall of ice.

Ice that overtakes some houses.
Perfect ice circle growing on some rivers.
Unusual snowing. Freak winter of terror.
Small mammals freeze where they stand.

RED HELL

You can do to a body a lot of things.
A *Smithsonian* feature on cannibalism makes me hungry.

I'm learning so much—to use bodies as ritual snacks,
eating everything but teeth, hair, and penis.

(Toenails, pills for stomachache.)

You can engage bodies with Aequanimitas
—emotional distance—as doctors do.

Or you can want them put down.
Eliminate 7,350,000/year to reach optimal population:

If they assume the fetal position,
they may be slaughtered in orderly fashion.

Make pain principles from anything: unripe papaya.
Pickle almost any man in a four-foot-tall glass jar.

Zip things in & out of bodies
surgically like a Sunday purse.

Stack sideways in walls, pour cement, build houses—
thumb your nose at haunting and good engineering.

I reckon cannibals use bodies like the rest of us:
radical application of questions ordinary or extraordinary.

(This is the worst way, the only natural way—in anger, add fuel.)

One lonely people-eater, upset by his son's truancy,
twice burned down his own treehouse.

BLUE HELL

A Sacramento City Council ordinance says: MOVE!
In response, a caravan of squatters crawls
10 inches at a time—*up* and *over*—

Then back before the hill breaks.
Barely any time to press the gas and rarely
Any fumes to feed the system of smoke

Breathed out from their sink-pit
Night after night as they talk about the best ways to live.
These men, these broke men:

Back & forth over law like a cradle,
Expecting everything to relapse
In a lot of rubbish, anyhow.

Trash is really enough now—breaching Space treaties.
Broken satellite bits slumming with astrotourists,
Planet of loam and litter flung in free choreography . . .

Annexing Antarctica—*sewage*, a study in ice.
The extra extra clean of crystalline right away melts to rot
As refuse rocks clear out of control.

HELL WITH THE LID OFF

Something thought to be cow,
sprinkled on commuters. Large mobs
of blackbirds slamming into signal towers—
lavished over simple sky, way in the West.

How lucky you'd have been to have been there.

Silhouettes organize into people plus accessories:
a project of billions preying upon one another
in extravagant ways. Three German tourists
have come to see the very ending of this world

—an illness both ancient and futuristic—

that is, the desire to be struck by disaster.
To live through a crash, lose everything in wildfire.
I might not survive this unkind apparatus of night,
but to prophesize death is to wish it,

uplighting and whimper.

—Yes, and all these things from the single drop of dire—

The new game is psychoball.

Bunkers for future
wars in hallucination monoculture:

tidy laboratory
with hint of machine.

Performance art collectives draped
in ghostwear.

Constant machine machinations in being
methodically crushed.

Plans for crash test theme parks, abandoned.

Graffiti not making sense . . . *not bad* but not finished.

Old,
regular train station.

My photojournals: —shot after shot—
in cold blood bed & breakfast.

Skies with stillborn suns.

The off-putting institution of entire life . . .

Life— & that *other* thing.

WHAT FRESH HELL IS *THIS*?

I.

You ask me:

"But how will I know it's you
when we meet in a future life?"

Everything is omen and all numbers relevant.
If you spot a man sweeping the entranceway
        and your eyes meet

and you feel mini flurries of a crush as he feels the same—

That's Me. Showing symptoms of generational curse:
bowl-headed and illiterate till 7, the Age of Salvation.
There at the funeral for some enemy of the state: You,

clever enough to be invited. I might be the cardinal.
I may weigh as much as a thousand lesser nightjars.
You will say you want to talk about God. I will say,

"We'll get to that."

II.

Psychologists reveal that while reading any text,
we adopt its belief and bias. Comics, the Bible,
this book—*your primer for my coming iteration*—
Learn that life is a terrible wrath to pass down!

In remakes of our lives, we are trapped in molds
cast when we were young and hated ourselves.
Observe some stranger to diagnose virility
and politics, how she handles a drink.

Like carrion crows or ravens, *rascals of the sky*,
identify all animals last seen near your dead
as possible dangers. Try to stay in the present,
which is bluegrass and prospects of violence.

Then the magnesium of the self,
uranium of who I really am.

Look at me to see a black rainbow of human vice.
You will know me by bushmeat-for-sex behaviors.
My classical *Unevolvia*. You will know me:
Mary-Alice, Sheepdog of Information.

III.

And this is why I can't get on board with reincarnation:
the next thing that always happens is . . . *We are ghoulish.*

We could have done good, but we chose
bad bad bad all the same all the way around.

Instead of *Do Not Resuscitate,* we really should leave
alternate instruction – *Please Do Not Reincarnate.*

Now repeat after me a prayer for no other lives forthcoming:

"I BEG PERMISSION TO RETURN
TO MY MOST FINAL DEATH.
GOOD NIGHT, PLANET EARTH.
GOOD LUCK, HUMANITY."

Nightwork

(Notes)

PICTOGRAMS

- The second illustration (page 23) features a *hamsa*. This symbol of a staring eye is seen throughout the Islamic world—a talisman warding off the evil eye, envy, ill will.
- The final hazard sign (page 95) cautions workers around machines with dangerous moving parts that start without warning: automatically and unexpectedly.

POEM NOTES (IN ORDER OF APPEARANCE)

- Epigraph: Quoted from Parul Sehgal's book review of *The Sexual Night* by Pascal Quignard, *New York Times*, December 5, 2014.
- "Revivalism 101": One line refers to laboratory rat experiments carried out in the 1960s. A behavioral scientist's rodent utopia spiraled into a self-destructing universe whose spoiled residents did nothing except "eat, sleep, and groom": Robert Brockway, "5 Sci-Fi Dystopias We've Actually Created (For Animals)," Cracked.com, June 13, 2012.
- "Slipstream": *Bone-house* is an Old English term for *body*. It also indicates a place to house the bones of your dead: an ossuary. The Dictionary of Obscure Sorrows website defines *onism* as "the frustration of being stuck in just one body, that inhabits only one place at a time." This website is artist John Koenig's brainchild; when it went viral in 2015, his etymologies of elusive emotions became as meaningful as Merriam-Webster. Koenig's definitions of universal human experiences impelled me away from inert alienation—for a moment.
- "Wolfmoon": My poem references Namwali Serpell, "The Zambian 'Afronaut' Who Wanted to Join the Space Race," *The New Yorker*, March 11, 2017. It also notes a post on the Historic Mysteries blog, "Overtoun Bridge: Where Dogs Leap to Their Deaths."
- "Ode to Our Unnamed Moon": A "dark star of calamity" is one way to describe the attraction to tragedy, according to a local newspaper editor after the Sandy Hook Elementary School shooting in 2013. The image of white moths recollects a taxidermy exhibit inside the Museum of

Jurassic Technology in Los Angeles. This cabinet of curiosities inspirits other images in the book, particularly those of animal experimentation and anatomy. *Note:* Neil Armstrong did *not* hear the call to prayer on the moon; this is only a persistent legend.

- "Nollywoodland": *Biblical reference*: 1 Peter 5:8 (King James): "Be sober, be vigilant; because your adversary the devil, as a roaring lion, walketh about, seeking whom he may devour."
- "Deathcentric": The final line adapts the title of a 2015 video posted on the White Wolf Pack blog (whitewolfpack.com), "Wild Ravens Frolic in Snow Like Children."
- "Chaos Muppet": This poem's title credits the Muppet Theory of human behavior explained by *Slate* writer Dahlia Lithwick. She conceptualizes our species as two opposite types: chaos muppets and order muppets. Chaos muppets are classically out of control. The Dictionary of Obscure Sorrows website defines *ellipsism* as the "sadness that you'll never be able to know how history will turn out, that you'll dutifully pass on the joke of being alive without ever learning the punchline." *Biblical references*: Job 7:3 (International Standard Version): "Truly I've been allotted months of emptiness; nights of trouble have been appointed for me." Lamentations 1:2 (King James): "Among all her lovers she hath none to comfort her: all her friends have dealt treacherously with her, they are become her enemies."
- "Indifferent Paradise": References Bob Pool, "City of Angels' First Name Still Bedevils Historians," *Los Angeles Times,* March 26, 2005.
- "Adios, LA . . .": My poem's title recalls bright billboards emblazoned with this farewell from Angeleno artist Jon Jackson when he abandoned LA for NYC in 2011. The Dictionary of Obscure Sorrows website defines *vemödalen* as "the frustration of photographing something amazing when thousands of identical photos already exist—the same sunset, the same waterfall."
- "For My Uncle Who Died of AIDS Contracted at the Dentist's Office": The title relates an actual event; my uncle had a toothache. All the epithets of Allah are accurate. *Qur'anic references*: Qur'an 2:156: "To Allah (Almighty God) we belong, and to Him is our return." Qur'an Surah Taha 20:55: "From this very earth We created you and to the same earth We shall cause you to return."
- "Zombi": The spelling of this poem's title points to the West African animism underlying the corrupted Western concept of zombies. In a mythos that traveled alongside the enslaved to the Americas and

became Vodun (*Vodou, voodoo*), a *zombi* is a spirit capable of reanimating a corpse.

- "Hyperreality": "A Shocking Sabbath Carnival of Death" was the sensational *New York Herald* headline on November 9, 1874. The front page reported 49 human killings following a mass animal escape from the Central Park Zoo—*the whole thing, a hoax.*
- "Nightmare": The cunning personalities of crows charmed me while reading Joseph Castro, "Grudge-Holding Crows Pass on Their Anger to Family and Friends," *Discover Magazine*, June 30, 2011.
- "Recurring Nightmare": The *Journal of Clinical Sleep Medicine* discusses nightmare drafting in its *Best Practice Guide for the Treatment of Nightmare Disorder in Adults.* The phrase "nightmares of murder in a small town" is quoted in Alex Kotlowitz's essay, "In the Face of Death," *New York Times Magazine*, July 6, 2003.
- "Why Does Dream Logic Always Work against You?": The maxim "Life is vortex, not rotation" paraphrases a 2012 YouTube video, "The Helical Model—Our Solar System Is a Vortex." Symbolic flower meanings in this poem are sourced from the New Language of Flowers website.
- "You Remain in Mefloquine Psychosis for Months": The term *greenbirds* refers to an Islamic metaphor for martyred souls as well as to a hashtag used by ISIS insurgents to glorify suicide bombers—from Sahih Muslim Book 20, Hadith 4651. The violin of disgrace was a medieval instrument of torture.
- "*At Last*, Enter the Castle of Mental & Physical Wellbeing": This poem shares the sentiment in Amber Barnes's headline "Small Pockets in Women's Jeans Are the Work of the Devil and You Can't Convince Me Otherwise," BuzzFeed.com, August 7, 2018.
- "Enquiry into the Location & Nature of Hell": This title is derived from *An Enquiry into the Nature and Place of Hell*, a clerical tome published in 1714 by Tobias Swinden. The phrase "long fall and fire" cites "Into Everlasting Fire," *The Economist*, December 22, 2012.
- "One Hell": The opening stanza incorporates information about innumerable hells from "Into Everlasting Fire," *The Economist*, with an image from Lamentations 2:19 (King James): "Arise, cry out in the night: in the beginning of the watches pour out thine heart like water before the face of the Lord."
- "Two Hell": Translations of the individual names assigned to each day of the French Revolution (Republican) calendar are sourced from the digital archives of the Fondation Napoléon. The final lines integrate

predictions from Futuretimeline.net—a website forecasting scientific and technological advancements—with entries in a listicle, "21 Biblical Weather Events [In Real Life]," Cracked.com, February 10, 2014.

- "Red Hell": This poem was informed by Paul Raffaele, "Sleeping with Cannibals," *Smithsonian Magazine*, September 2006. My closing couplet rephrases the author's profile of one flesh-eating firebug. "If they assume the fetal position, they may be slaughtered in orderly fashion" references a photographic caption in "The 8 Creepiest Places on Earth," Cracked.com, October 31, 2012.
- "Hell with the Lid Off": The Dictionary of Obscure Sorrows website defines *lachesism* as "the desire to be struck by disaster—to survive a plane crash, to lose everything in a fire, to plunge over a waterfall."
- "What Fresh Hell Is *This?*": The message "Goodnight Earth, goodnight humans" was the final transmission relayed to Earth in 2014 by the malfunctioning lunar rover named Jade Rabbit. The lines "You will say you want to talk about God. I will say, 'We'll get to that'" relate an interview conducted by Charles Bowden in "Sicario: A Juarez Hitman Speaks," *Harper's Magazine*, May 2009. One line in this poem was inspired by overhearing poet Gala Mukomolova asking, "Remember when we were young, when we hated ourselves?" Another, by professor Susan McCabe's joke: that humans should have the right to opt out of reincarnation.

dreamwork

My poetry feeds from my irregular experiences across Africa, America & England. Religious fusion and fervor long framed my life, even as I steadily turned skeptic. I was born in a *sharia state* near the border between Niger/Nigeria. My native tribe is >99 percent Islamic. The nomadic Fulani have been Muslim for a millennium—introducing Islam to much of West Africa beginning one thousand years ago, suppressing and synthesizing traditional polytheism. Most relatives desisted from idol and ancestor worship just one generation ago. Some summon gods in secret. Uncustomarily, both of my parents were ~~educated~~ indoctrinated within colonial Catholic, Lutheran, and Baptist missionary institutions. My Evangelical origin, an anomaly in the extreme north of Nigeria; you will not find another Mary-Alice in Maiduguri, city of my birth—also the birthplace of Boko Haram, the infamous terrorist militia. Regardless of religion, all lines of my family remain superstitious, passing down the residuum of spiritualities predating Christianity and Islam alike.

Myself, I mean to unseal an erratic inheritance—

so goes unruly alchemy, the dream world/our dread life.

Acknowledgments

EXPRESSIONS OF MY DEEPEST GRATITUDE TO:

Rae Armantrout—who gets it; who thankfully never expected "joy" from my work; who changed my life as a poet at the very moment I was ready to abandon it

Paul Corrigan—an indispensable editor and the best reader of my work

Jennifer Banks; Ash Lago; Caitlin Gallagher; Joyce Ippolito—for true kindness while helping me through every step of this overwhelming process

Jin Auh—for your exceptional energy, emotional intelligence, and advocacy

Kwame Dawes, Chris Abani, and Matthew Shenoda—for championing my work and making spaces for writers like me

Louise Glück; Bill Deresiewicz; Anne Fadiman; Laura Kasischke—for being the teachers and mentors who motivate me in the hope of one day making you proud

David St. John—for encouraging your students always; I'm sure none of us have found adequate words to express our appreciation

Airea Dee Matthews—whose magical presence in my MFA workshop *must* have had something to do with this miracle

Desiree Bailey—who after just one conversation became my North Star

Eduardo C. Corral and Robert Wood Lynn—for patient guidance as veterans

Suzanne Lummis—who pushed me to take greater poetic risks

Kenzie Allen—for entertaining my obsessive editorial meltdowns

Rosario Margate—who I know will be a lifelong collaborator

Shari Sharpe—for your absurdly generous gifts of time and talent

Uwani—for your selfless spirit and sacrifices

Ishaya—Having you as a big brother lends me strength.

Will Nguyen; Mel Campos; Reyna Camps; Juan Castillo; Nicole Diop—How do I deserve to have you as best friends? *I don't.* Thank you for loving me, anyway.

Safiya Sinclair—I had to give you your own line, bestie. Your incandescent light lifts me.

Mommy—You're the greatest blessing in my lifetime. "Many women do noble things, but you surpass them all" (Proverbs 31:29).

SPECIAL RECOGNITION
My dearest friend, Juan Castillo, a Los Angeles–based graphic artist, designed the six warning signs and symbols within this book.

Versions or segments of certain poems in this volume have appeared in the following publications, and I sincerely thank the editors:

MAGAZINES: *Anti-, American Poetry Review, Black Warrior Review, Callaloo, Hayden's Ferry Review, Indiana Review, Los Angeles Review of Books, Connotation Press, Meridian, Mid-American Review, New England Review, New Orleans Review, Nimrod International Journal, Cutthroat, Painted Bride Quarterly, PANK, Superstition Review, Tampa Review, The Iowa Review, Waxwing, Word Riot*

ANTHOLOGIES: *Best New Poets (University of Virginia Press); Wide Awake: Poets of Los Angeles and Beyond (Beyond Baroque Books); Furious Flower: Seeding the Future of African American Poetry (Northwestern University Press)*

CHAPBOOK SERIES: *New-Generation African Poets (Akashic Books)*